GOLF GOLF GOLF

OTHER BOOKS BY S. GROSS

How Gross

I Am Blind and My Dog Is Dead

An Elephant Is Soft and Mushy

More Gross

Why Are Your Papers in Order?

Dogs Dogs Dogs

Cats Cats Cats

All You Can Eat

WITH JAMES CHARLTON

Books Books Books

GOLF GOLF GOLF

A Hilarious Collection of Cartoons

Edited by S. Gross

1817

HARPER & ROW, PUBLISHERS, New York
Grand Rapids, Philadelphia, St. Louis, San Francisco
London, Singapore, Sydney, Tokyo

To Irv and Ellie—a couple of golf nuts

Grateful acknowledgment is made for permission to reprint the following:

Cartoon on page 124 by Donald Reilly in *Playboy*. Copyright 1983 by *Playboy*. Reproduced by special permission of *Playboy* Magazine.

Cartoons copyrighted by *The New Yorker* are indicated throughout the book.

Some of the cartoons in this collection have appeared in the following periodicals and are reprinted by permission of the authors: Diversion, El Mundo, Family Circle, Fore, Friends Magazine, Golf Digest, Good Housekeeping, Parade, Plain Dealer, Saturday Evening Post, Scouting.

FIRST EDITION

Designer: Kim Llewellyn

LIBRARY OF CONGRESS CATALOG CARD NUMBER 88-45971
ISBN 0-06-016126-4

89 90 91 92 93   HOR   10 9 8 7 6 5 4 3 2 1

"You're going to shoot
a hundred and fourteen, dear."

2

3

4

5

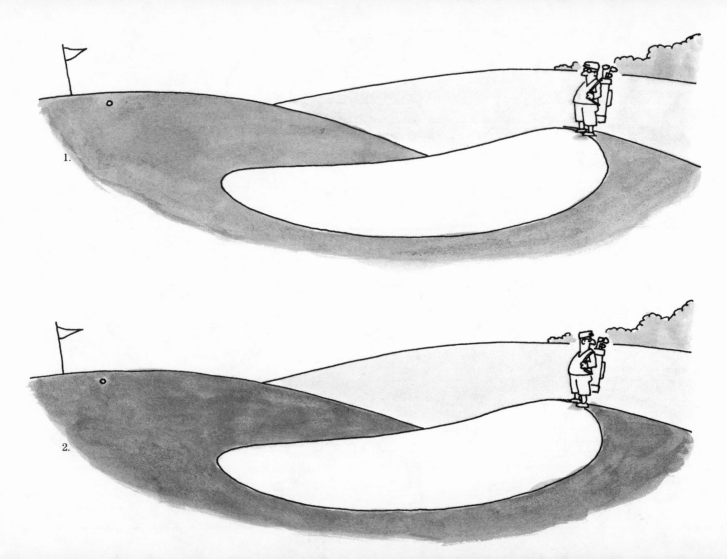

1.

2.

3.

4.

JACK ZIEGLER

7

"Your grip is okay, but your stance is a little wide."

"Chip's feet were cold."

ORLANDO BUSINO

9

"He's not having a good day. He shot his age this morning."

"Be careful of that grass trap, Akim."

NICK DOWNES

ED FRASCINO

"I'll let you know where to send the rest of my things."

"Teeing off early?"

In search of the missing links.

MICHAEL MASLIN

ORLANDO BUSINO

16

"I don't know, 'fore' hardly seems adequate."

18

"Believe me, when we get back, I'm going to have a word with
the Green's Committee!"

BILL WOODMAN

19

"I wasn't talking to you. I was talking to my nine iron."

ED FRASCINO

JOHN JONIK

21

Dedini

ELDON DEDINI

M.E. COHEN

CONDOMS FOR GOLFERS

23

"Mr. Sammett's caddie just called to say he's stuck in a sand trap on the ninth green."

MIKE TWOHY

"Nasty slice you've got there!"

FELIPE GALINDO (FEGGO)

"Every day they get a new hazard on this course."

ORLANDO BUSINO

27

28   David slew Goliath with a great "swing," not "sling," as previously reported.

JOHN JONIK

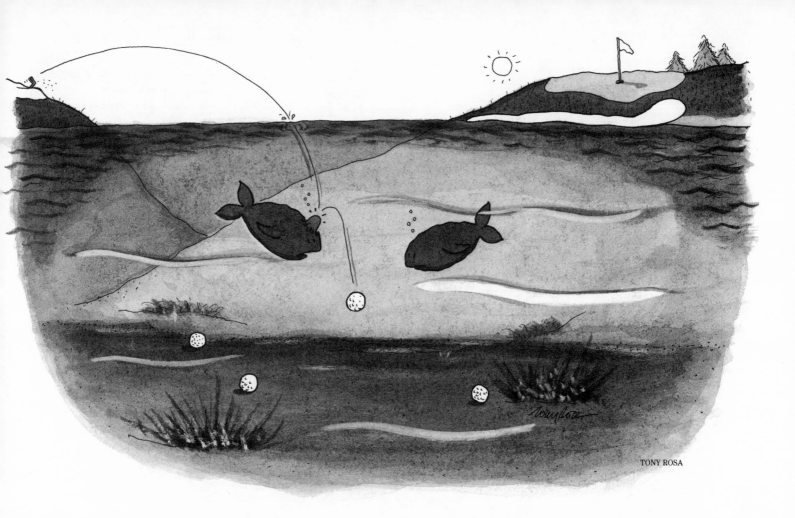

"I miss the fish tank in the clubhouse."

TONY ROSA

29

JERRY MARCUS

ED FRASCINO

31

DAVID JACOBSON

"I guess it's that time of year again."

NORT GERBERG

"Nevertheless, I'd feel better if we played a little faster."

JOHN JONIK

35

CHARLES SAUERS

"Someone with our name is winning the U.S. Open!"

HENRY MARTIN

"Do you, Helen, with a handicap of 9, take Clifford, with a handicap of 7...."

OUT OF BOUNDS

JOHN DEMPSEY

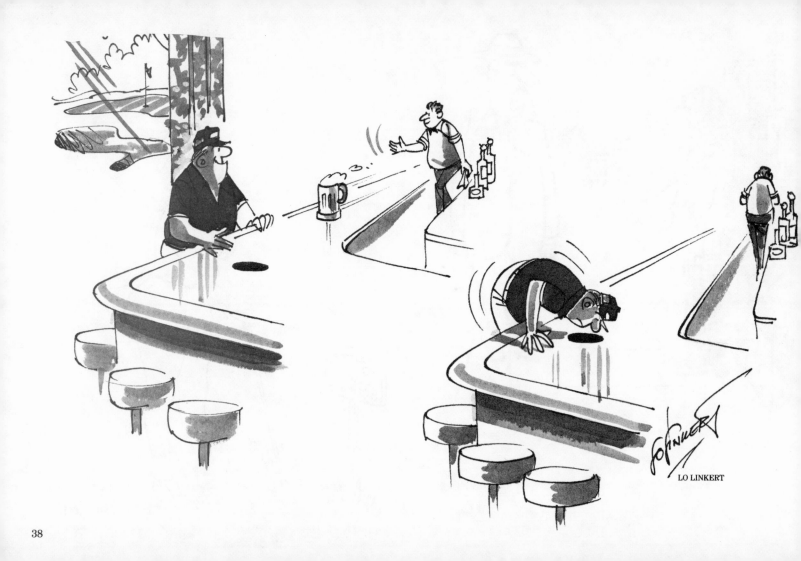

LO LINKERT

BILL MAUL

"The tower says your blind shot out of the woods is no more than three feet from the pin.... The bad news is, the lake's only about *two* feet from the pin."

39

ELI BAUER

MARTY MURPHY

"—Why, yes, Mrs. Feeny—In fact, I have your file in front of me right now."

LEO CULLUM

"Triple bogey."

STEWART
STEWART SLOCUM

WILLIAM MAUL

CHARLES SAXON

"There's no use wasting the day sulking. Why don't you get out your nice new fountain pen and write some thank-you notes?"

EVERETT OPIE

"Amigos, do you mind if the Premier plays through?"

"What makes you so sure he's a hustler?"

"Excuse me. Did you happen to see a 'Patton Penfold' skitter by?"

DON DOUGHTERTY

47

MEL YAUK

1.

2.

3.

JOHN DEMPSEY

"Still too much backswing. Hold your left arm
straighter. Keep your head…"

49

50

51

The Island of Lost Balls

REVILO

OLIVER CHRISTIANSON (REVILO)

"Look, I'll make you a deal. I'll get my flock to patronize your place if you get your flock to patronize my place."

53

FRANK
RIDGEWAY

FRANK RIDGEWAY

"He's the only person to pay his membership dues on time."

WOODMAN

BILL WOODMAN

"What's this I hear about you giving up golf photography?"

JERRY MARCUS

59

"That's it? 'Keep my head down?'"

JERRY MARCUS

"I can't find my life jacket."

"He got up one morning eight years ago and said he was going to
take a Mulligan in the game of life. I haven't seen him since."

MARTY MURPHY

PORGES

PETER PORGES

"Leave my master alone!"

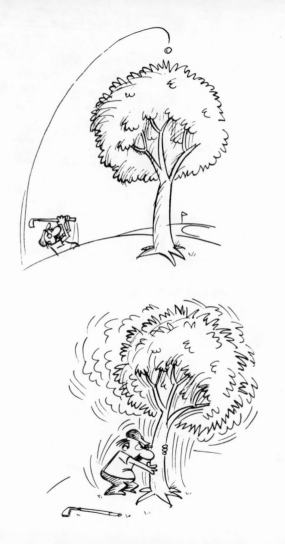

ARTURO POTTIER

65

BERNARD SCHOENBAUM

"All my life I have wondered about the river Styx. It's roughly about a five iron, wouldn't you say?"

BRIAN SAVAGE

DICK OLDDEN

"If you knew you had to replace your divots, Herbert, why didn't you do it?"

HARA-KIRI

Sauers

CHARLES SAUERS

"Where did we go wrong, Alice?"

"It's my husband! Damn! He must have missed the cut!"

MARTY MURPHY

BRIAN SAVAGE

"Internal Revenue Service! Pull over!"

OLDDEN
DICK OLDDEN

"Mind if we play through?"

CATHERINE O'NEILL

75

"I hope we're not going to go through this *every* time you get a hole in one."

DON OREHEK

"You would think that up here, on the last hole, they would let you keep the ball."

BILL MAUL

©CASSADY

JOHN CASSADY

"IV!"

"The doctor is going to give you a shot. By the time you wake up, I'll be back."

1.

2.

3.

4.

5.

6.

ARAGONÈS
SERGIO ARAGONES

83

BRIAN
SAVAGE

BRIAN SAVAGE

"Yes, it *is* remarkable, I suppose. But the important thing is that he can drop another ball and not be penalized a stroke."

STEWART

STEWART SLOCUM

"Next!"

84

"Oh, for goodness' sake, forget it, Beasley. Play another one."

VAHAN SHIRVANIAN

"Happy birthday. You said you liked to shoot golf."

CLEM SCALZITTI

"You've never kissed me like that!"

BRIAN SAVA

"I know 217 is a helluva lot for nine holes, Lou, but I also think your caddie left a great deal to be desired."

"That reminds me....Did you pack my golf shoes?"

MARTY MURPHY

89

"Of course I can make a commitment. I'm committed to my job, I'm committed to the Constitution and I'm committed to my golf game."

JOE MIRACHI

"Thank you, God of Golf!"

AL ROSS

BERNARD SCHOENBAUM

ELDON DEDINI

"No matter *how* I treated you, Julia, haunting a man at golf
is hitting below the belt."

BOOK OF
WORLD
RECORDS

SCHWADRON
HARLEY SCHWADRON

93

CHARLES SAXON

"You're getting cold."

BRIAN SAVAGE

"I thought the Supreme Court outlawed that!"

"What kind of nut would be out fishing in this weather?"

ORLANDO BUSINO

95

BERNARD SCHOENBAUM

AL ROSS

S. GROSS

S. GROSS

"Beat it! I don't need a personal demon
when I'm playing golf."

98

AL ROSS

DON OREHEK

"This happens every time we pass the golf course."

LO LINKERT

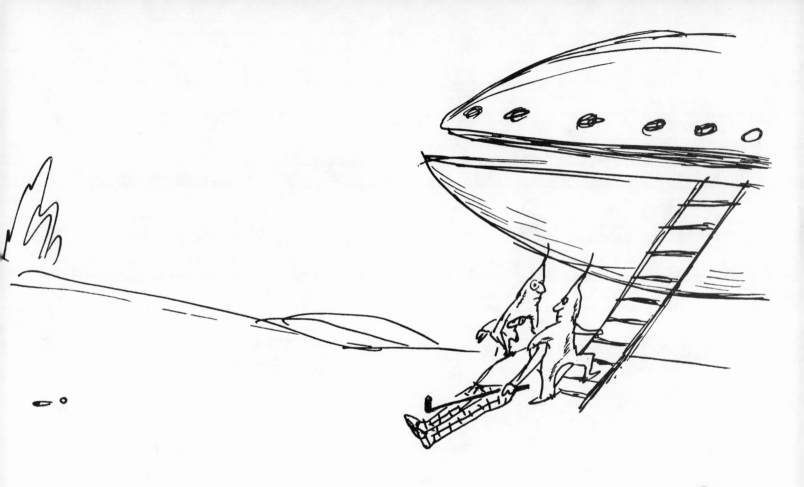

"*Please*, fellows! For God's sake, let me finish the hole!
I've got an *eagle* coming up!"

AL ROSS

LO LINKERT

"I'd like golf better if they allowed a designated putter."

ARTEMIS COLE

"I'm on a golf kick. When he mentions golf, I kick him!"

"The roof, please."

JONIK
JOHN JONIK

POLLS

GEO LEVINE
GEORGE LEVINE

"The world's greatest invention? I'd say it was those
orange golf balls."

ARTEMIS COLE

"This is for Joan Flaherty. She beat the boss at golf today."

JOHN JONIK

MANNY CURTIS

"It's a rare form of athlete's foot that only golfers get."

S. GROSS

"Remember, son, it isn't whether you win or lose, it's how you cheat at the game."

NICK DOWNES

"At least you cleared the spent-fuel pond."

CHARLES SAUERS

"Hang in there, Harry—we'll have you out of this in no time."

MEL YAUK

BRIAN SAVAGE

"I know what you're doing back there, you filthy swine."

DON OREHEK

"I've been here since '81. I hate to think what this has done to my golf game."

JOSEPH FARRIS

109

BRIAN SAVAGE

"Tell me when."

ED FRASCINO

"Fair warning, Randal. I'm this close to becoming
a golf widow for real."

AARON BACALL

"I know it's hard for you to understand how I feel…
but you don't know the course."

ARTEMIS COLE

"You broke 100? Are you on steroids or something?"

"Stop *watching* me!"

BILL MAUL

"I've heard of elevated greens before, but this is ridiculous!"

"It says that he found the game of golf inspiring at the expense
of it being relaxing."

OLDDEN

DICK OLDDEN

114

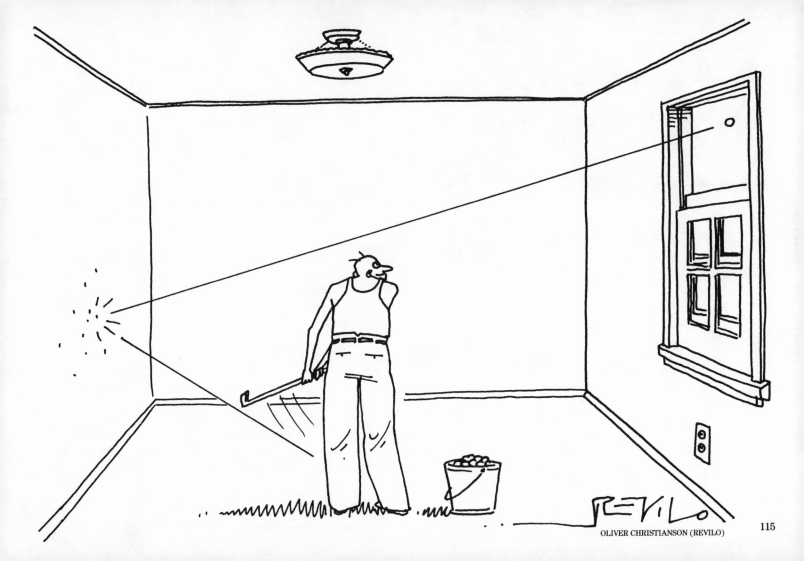

OLIVER CHRISTIANSON (REVILO)

115

ALL CADDIES REPORT IMMEDIATELY TO THE FIRST TEE!

BRIAN SAVAGE

AARON BACALL

"I'll look for the ball. You look for the club."

117

"I wouldn't mind her taking that much time putting, but my babysitter costs me a fortune."

119

120

PHIL INTERLANDI

"That's Harry's problem. He's all lessons and no game."

121

GOLFBALLS THE SIZE OF HAILSTONES

JACK ZIEGLER

"A large bucket of balls and a gag!"

DON OREHEK

123

CHARLES SAUERS

"Gosh, Gilliam, it's only golf."

DONALD REILLY